THE EMPEROR
AKBAR'S
KHAMSA OF NIẒĀMĪ

THE EMPEROR
AKBAR'S
KHAMSA OF NIẒĀMĪ

Barbara Brend

THE BRITISH LIBRARY

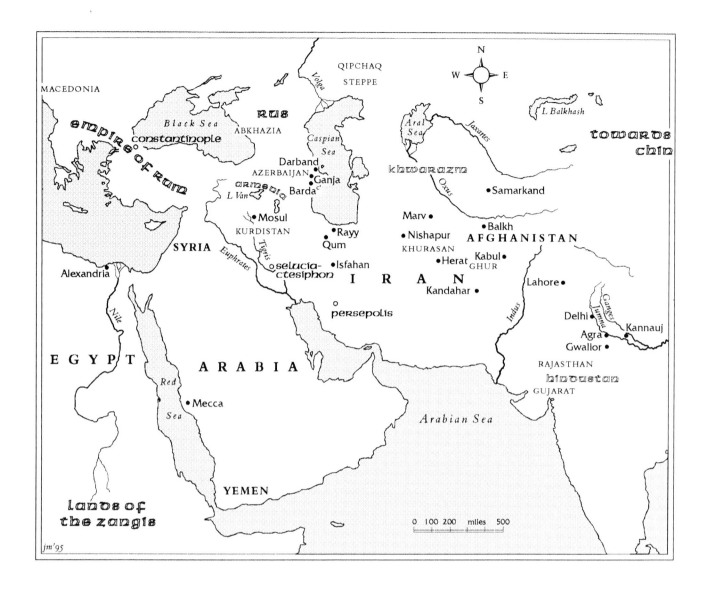

To Norah M. Titley, who opened my eyes to Persian painting,
and Professor T. Gandjeī, who opened my ears to Persian poetry.

Thanks are due to the Walters Art Gallery, Baltimore, for permission to
reproduce their pictures. I should also like to express my gratitude for
help given to me by staff of the British Library, especially Janet Backhouse,
Jeremiah P. Losty, Muhammad Isa Waley, and David Way.

Barbara Brend, 1995

First published 1995 by The British Library
Great Russell Street, London WC1B 3DG

© in text 1995, Barbara Brend

ISBN 0–7123–0392–8

Designed by James Shurmer

Colour origination by York House Graphics, Hanwell

Typeset in Linotype Bembo by Bexhill Phototypesetters

Printed in England by Clifford Press, Coventry

THE EMPEROR AKBAR'S *KHAMSA* OF NIẒĀMĪ

One of the most splendid manuscripts produced for the sixteenth-century Mughal emperor Akbar is a richly illustrated copy of a classical Persian work, the *Khamsa* or 'Quintet' of the twelfth-century poet Niẓāmī.

Akbar

The British Library's manuscript was made for Akbar, who reigned in northern India from 1556–1605 and was a patron of manuscripts on a prodigious scale. The greatest calligraphers of the day and more than two hundred painters worked in his palace studio. The Mughal dynasty was descended from Tīmūr, a Turk of Central Asia, where Islam was the accepted faith, who founded an empire with Samarkand as capital in the late fourteenth century, and died in 1405. Tīmūr's descendant, Bābur, captured Delhi in 1526 and formed a kingdom in North India, based on Agra; Bābur's son, Humāyūn, was forced to flee in 1540 and, having sought help in Iran, ruled in Kabul, in present-day Afghanistan, until he was able to regain the Indian lands in 1555. Akbar, Humāyūn's son, succeeded in 1556; he was able to extend his territory, and then to a considerable extent to reconcile his Hindu subjects. In the sphere of painting Akbar could exploit the talents of artists trained in Iran and acquired by his father, and of Hindu painters who may have served in the courts of the Rajput chiefs he defeated. Another source of stylistic ideas, perhaps transmitted by a sprinkling of actual painters, was from the Muslim courts of pre-Mughal India; and in addition, in the course of Akbar's reign, a number of European works came to hand. Painting in Akbar's day was predominantly, but not exclusively, the illustration of manuscripts. In his youth Akbar favoured adventurous or comic stories, but from the late 1580s, and probably with a view to asserting the legitimacy of Mughal power, he turned more frequently to histories. Among these were the memoirs of his grandfather Bābur, translated from the Chaghaṭāy Turkish of Central Asia into Persian, and known as the *Bāburnāma* (The Story of Bābur). At about the same period, Akbar began to commission copies of some of the great classics of Persian literature: among them a *Khamsa* of Niẓāmī, produced in 1595, when the Mughal court was resident in Lahore.

Niẓāmī

The poet Abū Muḥammad Ilyās ibn Yūsuf ibn Mu'ayyad, known by the pen-name of Niẓāmī, lived in North-Western Iran in the late twelfth century. The epithet Ganja'ī or Ganjavī associates him with the town of Ganja in the Republic of Azerbaijan and, though it is not certain this was his birthplace, he appears to have spent most of his life there. At this period Iran was in political turmoil: the power of the Saljūq (Seljuk) Turks, overlords since the mid-eleventh century, was breaking down, and minor princes or local lords – *atābegs*, formerly governors for the Saljūqs – were seeking to establish themselves. As was customary, Niẓāmī dedicated his works to various such princes and lords.

There is some doubt as to the precise dates of Niẓāmī's life and works. It is probable that he was born in 535/1140–41; the date of his death is less certain, but it may be 605/1208–9. His father was from Qum, in Iran, and his mother a Kurd. He was orphaned young and brought up by an uncle, receiving a wide education influenced by the mystical trends of the time. He married three times, but was most attached to his first wife, Āfāq, a Qipchāq slave, and thus of Turkish origin.

The Khamsa

The *Khamsa* is a quintet of books; it is written in rhyming couplets known as *masnavī*. Nizami's quintet consists of a didactic work and four romances, whose heroes have a historical origin. *Makhzan al-Asrār* (The Treasury of Secrets), probably composed

Fig.1 *Sanjar and the old woman*, f.15b
(No. 2, La‘l).

6

between 1155 and 1166, contains twenty moral discourses, each of which is followed by a brief parable to illuminate its meaning. *Khusraw va Shīrīn* (Khusraw and Shīrīn), is datable between 1176 and 1186; it tells the loves of Khusraw II Parvīz (590–628), a king of the Sasanian dynasty, that ruled Iran before the Arab conquest, and Shīrīn, a princess of Armenia. It has been suggested that Niẓāmī modelled the noble and independent character of Shīrīn on that of his wife Āfāq. *Laylā va Majnūn* (Laylā and Majnūn), completed in Rajab 584/late September 1188, is the tragic story of two lovers from different tribes in Arabia. *Haft Paykar* (The Seven Beauties), completed on 14 Ramażān 593/31 July 1197, is a narrative which frames seven shorter tales; its principal hero is the Sasanian king Bahrām V (420–38), known as Bahrām Gūr, from his passion for hunting the wild ass (*gūr*). *Iskandarnāma* (The Story of Iskandar) follows the Persian tradition for the deeds of Alexander the Great; it is in two parts, sometimes called *Sharafnāma* and *Iqbālnāma*. The first part may have been completed before the *Haft Paykar*; the second part was probably in progress about 1202.

Fig.2 *Farīdūn and the gazelle*, f.19a
(No. 3, Mukund).

The Manuscript

Without exception it is the most wonderful Indian manuscript in Europe, not only for its unsurpassed beauty and its profuse gold borders, but also on account of its marvellous state of preservation.

F. R. Martin, 1912

Many copies of the *Khamsa*, whether illustrated or not, were produced down the centuries for Persian-speaking rulers, and indeed the British Library's manuscript (Or. 12208) is not the first made in Akbar's studio. The British Library volume was copied by the fortieth year of Akbar's reign in 1004/1595, probably in Lahore where Akbar was then resident, and is the work of Akbar's foremost scribe ʿAbd al-Raḥīm. It now contains 37 illustrated folios, which produce 36 narrative illustrations, since one is a double-page composition; there is also a picture showing ʿAbd al-Raḥīm at work, added on the final colophon page in the time of Akbar's son Jahāngīr. The manuscript was bought in 1909 by C. W. Dyson Perrins, who, dying in 1958, bequeathed it to the British Museum; whence it came to the British Library, when the latter was established in 1973. It is in good, but not pristine condition. At some time prior to the 1909 sale a portion of the work was extracted, and this is now in the Walters Art Gallery, Baltimore. The illustrated folios of this portion, published in 1960 by S. C. Welch, are five in number, but they contribute only four further narrative subjects, since again there is a double-page. The Walters pictures will here be notionally reinstated in their places in the narrative, the total of 42 illustrated folios yielding 40 subjects. The outermost border of the folios in the British Library manuscript is a meander, while some of the Walters Art Gallery pictures have a border of loops and finials; both must result from refurbishment, perhaps performed just prior to the sale in 1909.

Below the narrative pictures are ascriptions to a score of artists of Akbar's workshop, and these are accompanied by running numbers from one to 44 (double-pages counting as two). Numbers 27 and 28 are missing, presumably from the beginning of the *Iskandarnāma*, so that the total of illustrated subjects was originally 42, or 41 if the missing folios formed a double-page. The names and numbers, written in a minute hand, appear to be the authentic work of a Mughal librarian. The numbers raise a curious problem, since they run in sequence, in spite of the fact that some illustrations are out of the usual narrative order, *Khusraw va Shīrīn* having one unusual placing and *Laylā va Majnūn* several. The order of the folios is further confirmed by catchwords, which announce at the foot of one page the first word of the next, and which appear to be original. It therefore looks as though the order of the illustrations dates from the origin of the manuscript and not from later disturbance, but whether it is the result of error or deliberate choice remains mysterious.

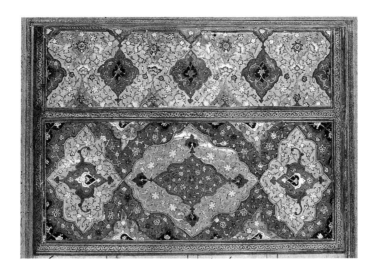

Makhzan al-Asrār

As is customary, the book opens with the praise of God, followed by that of the Prophet Muḥammad; then come literary discussion, and praise of the patron.

Following the *Second Discourse: on justice and the maintenance of equity*, the first illustration is *Nūshīrvān and his vizier* (No. 1, Manohar; frontispiece). Nūshīrvān goes hunting one day and, accompanied only by his vizier, rides far from his followers. He sees a ruined village in which are perched two birds deep in conversation, and he asks his vizier what they are talking about. Begging the king to accept a lesson, the vizier explains that the birds are discussing a marriage. The one requires that this ruined village be given as a dowry; the other replies that, if the king continues in his tyrannous way, he will soon be in a position to provide five thousand such ruined villages. Nūshīrvān is distraught; he laments and gallops back to his followers. He lifts his heavy taxes and removes injustices.

The Sasanian ruler Nūshīrvān, or Anūshīrvān, the Just, ruled Iran from 531 to 579; the story illustrates the fact that it was a delicate matter to present criticism to powerful ancient kings. The painter Manohar often likes to focus attention on a single significant gesture. Nūshīrvān's right hand indicates the village and the birds – here, as was customary, interpreted as owls – while he turns his head to his vizier to put the question. The yellow ground against which the courtly characters are shown distances them from the more shady green of the rest. A bridge continues the line of the king's gesture, leading the eye into the ruins. The scene is enlivened by jackals, birds, and the eager hunting-dog. Though the jackals at least are to be associated with the ruined condition of the village, the animation of the animals implies that decay is not inevitable. As is frequently the case in Mughal painting of this period, the background shows the influence of Western manuscript painting of the fifteenth or early sixteenth century in the treatment of buildings, and in the reduced size and delicate application of paint to convey distance. It is known that a Jesuit mission brought pictures to Akbar in 1580, though European sources seem to have been used before that; further Jesuit missions came in 1591 and 1595. The subject may have been selected for the first illustration to associate Akbar with

Nūshīrvān, who brings justice out of disorder; the second picture takes up the same theme.

The *Fourth Discourse: on the proper treatment of subjects* is followed by *Sultan Sanjar and the old woman* (No. 2, Laᶜl; fig. 1). An old woman appeals to Sultan Sanjar saying that a drunken watchman has mishandled her and shamed her by accusing her of harbouring a murderer in her house. Sanjar, she says, has thrown the world into turmoil; the empire of his Turkish forebears was founded on justice, but he is not true to this ideal.

Sanjar, a Saljūq, governed Khurasan (Eastern Iran) from 1097 to 1157, engaging in combat with external forces and members of his own family. It may be that the painter Laᶜl intends to express the extent of Sanjar's lordship by the wide landscape with a walled city, which he indicates behind the principal figures; while the entourage, royal parasol, and royal weapons in their carrying bags are symbols of power. Attention is called to the centre of the picture by the enveloping white *burqaᶜ* of the old woman. Laᶜl reveals his feeling for people in her posture, both urgent and dignified, as she leans forward to catch the sultan's sash. Free access to the ruler for the redress of grievances was an ancient Persian concept, though perhaps more honoured in the breach than the observance.

The *Seventh Discourse: on the superiority of man to animals*, is followed by *Farīdūn and the gazelle* (No. 3, Mukund; fig. 2). Hunting one day with a few companions, Farīdūn sees a gazelle which pleases him. Its neck and ear disarm hostility, and its eye and croup seemed to intercede for it; so intensely does it fascinate the king that it seems as though it were his own creation. Farīdūn sets his horse in pursuit while preparing his bow, but the arrow flies wide, and the speeding horse cannot attain the dust the gazelle sets up. Farīdūn asks his arrow and horse why they have failed. The arrow replies it could not strike that on which the king has set his eye.

Farīdūn is a virtuous king of Iran, whose story is found in the earlier and legendary part of the *Shāhnāma* (The Epic of the Kings), completed by the poet Firdawsī about 1010. Niẓāmī's brief story exploits the ambiguity of Persian poetical metaphor; ostensibly about hunting, it derives a certain tension from the fact that a gazelle may signify a beautiful woman. The moral which Niẓāmī appends to the story is not, in fact, to do with the relative importance of man and animals, but with the loyalty which the servant will show a king by serving his long-term interest, rather than his temporary whim.

The story is not usually illustrated and may have been selected as a third statement on the relations of a king and his subjects. Hunting, however, is a frequent subject – a similar scene is found on the manuscript's back cover – and Mukund is clearly happy to portray the spirited action of the chase, rather than to seek out the meaning of this particular text. The speed and élan of Farīdūn, picked out in red and rising in his stirrups, is emphasized by contrast with the slower movement of hunt-servants in the opposite direction. The quarry is blackbuck. The wide background, set back behind a *chinār* tree (oriental plane), includes a broad waterway, which contributes to the freshness of the scene. A fanciful touch is a peacock displaying to a peahen on a pinnacle of rock.

The fourth illustration turns on the dramatic interest of poison and the power of suggestion. The *Twelfth Discourse: on bidding farewell to this world* is followed by *The disputing physicians* (No. 4, Miskīna; fig. 3). Two physicians of the same school quarrel because each claims superiority. One night they agree to contest in courage and in skill.

Fig.3 *The disputing physicians*, f.23b (No. 4, Miskīna).

The one makes a potion of deadly poison. The other drinks it followed by an antidote of herbs. He then picks a rose and, breathing a spell over it, offers it to his opponent. The first, overcome by terror of the enchanted flower, falls dead.

The figures in this interior scene are larger in the picture than heretofore, and drawn with great confidence. Miskīna unites a feeling for the volumes of the human body, traceable in Indian art from the earliest periods onwards, with ideas from European manuscript painting or prints; specifically, for the expiring physician, he may have worked from the Christ of a *Deposition*. Such a picture could have been among those brought by the Jesuits; the wall-paintings may reflect these or other acquisitions. In one an archangel delivers a text to a sage; below this, in *grisaille*, and thus presumably from a print, a mythological female extends a scroll to another; in a third, a religious theme almost fades into secular decorative art as *putti* tramp the vintage. The fatal flower seems to be frangipani.

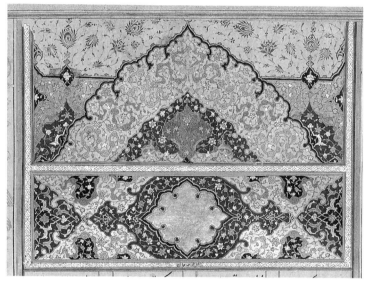

f.32b

Khusraw va Shīrīn

Hurmuz comes to the throne of Iran and rules with justice. He has a son, Khusraw Parvīz (Victorious Emperor), who shows brilliant early promise. The prince is instructed by a wise and learned man named Buzurg Umīd (Great Hope).

To prepare a well-ordered kingdom for his son, Hurmuz decrees that various misdemeanours shall be punished, but Khusraw himself falls foul of the decree. When out hunting, the prince alights at a village and passes a night of music and carousal with his companions. As dawn breaks, his horse snatches some of the green crop and a page steals some clusters of grapes. This is reported to the king, who, in spite of his son's involvement, orders that the horse's hoofs be cut off, that the page be given to the owner of the vineyard, that Khusraw's throne be given to the master of the house where he had lodged, and that the nails of his harper be broken. Later, Khusraw presents himself as a penitent before his father and is forgiven.

(*Right*) Fig.4 *Khusraw carouses*, f.40b (No. 5, Dharmdās).

(*Below, left*) Fig.5 *Shāpūr before Shīrīn*, f.45b (No. 6, Mādhū).

(*Below, right*) Fig.6 *Shāpūr brings Khusraw news of Shīrīn*, f.52a (No. 7, Dharmdās).

Fig. 7 *Khusraw honoured by his subjects*, f. 54a (No. 8, Narsingh).

Fig. 8 *Khusraw and Shīrīn meet on the hunting field*, f. 63b (No. 9, Nānhā).

We do not know whether Akbar himself selected the subjects for illustration in his manuscript, but it seems certain that any selection would have needed his approval. This being so, the rare subject *Khusraw carouses* (No. 5, Dharmdās; fig. 4) may have been chosen because it takes up the theme of royal justice, or perhaps because it concerns the relations of fathers and sons, a topic found in several illustrations later in the manuscript. However, if any warning to Akbar's sons was intended, it is not reflected in the work of the painter Dharmdās. Though the transgressions of the page and the horse are shown, and though musicians and wine-cups are included, the atmosphere is rather decorous. Far from disturbing the peace of a village, the prince seems about to receive a book which, from the clerical clothing of the donor, might be a work of edifying literature. If Dharmdās is constrained by the risks of implying criticism of a young prince, he revels in the opportunity to produce a luscious scene. The vine-trellis, greenery, water and wine suggest refreshment, and set off the bright clothes of courtiers and the sumptuous textiles used for Khusraw's robe (*jāma*) and for his horse's trappings. The large dark tree derives from the Hindu painting tradition, which would lay down a patch of dark colour and draw large leaves upon it; the vine-trellis seems to be from a European source.

Following this event, Khusraw's grandfather, Anūshīrvān (Nūshīrvān), appears to him in a dream and tells him that, since he has accepted the 'sour grapes' of his punishment, he will gain a beautiful lady, a horse named Shabdīz (Colour of Night), the throne, and

Fig.9 *Shīrīn entertains Khusraw*, f.65a (No. 10, Farrukh Chela and Dhanrāj).

a minstrel named Bārbad. Shāpūr, a companion of the prince, tells him of Shamīrā, known as Mihīn Bānū (Great Lady), who rules in Armenia, and of her niece, the chaste and beautiful Shīrīn (Sweet), beside whom the moon appears a mere beauty-spot. He also mentions that Mihīn Bānū has an exceptional horse named Shabdīz. Khusraw is captivated by the idea of Shīrīn and sends Shāpūr to Armenia to seek her out. When Shāpūr reaches the flowering upland pastures that Shīrīn visits with her maidens, he catches her attention by hanging Khusraw's picture in a tree three times, and so brings himself to Shīrīn's notice and contrives to speak to her.

Shāpūr before Shīrīn (No. 6; Mādhū; fig. 5) should properly be set in the open countryside, for if Shāpūr could gain admittance to the palace, the pictures of Khusraw would not have been necessary; and Shāpūr, the experienced courtier and artist, might be expected to be older than the messenger shown here. This young and bashful figure is, however, of very courtly appearance: the narcissus in his turban symbolizes the eyes of a lover and proclaims his romantic mission. While avoiding looking the princess in the face, Shāpūr 'bites the finger of surprise', a conventional gesture used in a variety of situations, and here perhaps showing amazement at Shīrīn's beauty and shyness in her presence. Shīrīn is shown as truly in command of the situation, beautiful, at ease and authoritative. As would have been the case at the Mughal court, the costumes of India and of Central Asia are both represented. Shīrīn wears a *jāma*, woven in the Indian tradition of transparent fineness, and trousers, but her headdress is of Central Asian type. Her older attendants wear this headdress and a gown, which must have been the costume of Mughal ladies born in Central Asia or Afghanistan. The younger attendants are shown either as Hindus or as Mughal ladies who have adopted Hindu costume. The seclusion of the courtly scene is emphasized by servants of different ranks outside the walls: door-guard and groom in the foreground; men toiling at a draw-well in the background. The portrayal of female figures raises the interesting question as to how the painter – a man, as painters of the workshop usually were – derived his view of courtly ladies. Would he see them or glimpse them about the palace? If not, would the women of his own family provide adequate models or information? Whatever the precise answers, the portrayal is convincing and consistent with those in other Mughal paintings.

At Shāpūr's suggestion, Shīrīn borrows Shabdīz and, on the pretext of hunting, she rides towards Madā'in (Seleucia-Ctesiphon, the Sasanian capital) to seek out Khusraw. He, however, has already left for Armenia to find her, and indeed, on the way he passes her while she is bathing in a pool, though he does not fully realise whom he has seen. Shīrīn arrives, and a small castle is built for her in a very hot region towards Kirmanshah (in Persian Kurdistan). In Armenia, Khusraw is well received by Mihīn Bānū, and he establishes a comfortable camp.

Khusraw is ensconced in his tent – the text tells us with music, wine and a brazier – when he is told that Shāpūr asks for admittance. *Shāpūr brings Khusraw news of Shīrīn* (No. 7, Dharmdās; cover and fig. 6) conveys the eagerness of the messenger with his speaking gestures; while the dreamy look of the plumpish prince suggests that a vision of Shīrīn is floating before his eyes. Dharmdās uses a composition similar to that in his *Khusraw carouses*. Here the surrounding tent-wall (*sarā-parda*) serves to keep the attendants at a distance from the prince, and its entrance is guarded by a black eunuch. The royal tent is of the frame variety, similar in structure to those of the nomads of Central Asia, its wall a cylindrical lattice, its domical roof formed by struts fitted to a central wheel. Instead of the felt of a nomad tent, the roof is covered with a rich brocade. Descended from nomads, the Mughals were accustomed to using tents as they moved about the country, and even in more permanent residences they raised elaborate tented structures for particular ceremonials.

Shāpūr conducts Shīrīn back to Armenia, but Khusraw is no longer there, since the death of his father has obliged him to return to Madā'in. At this point, the manuscript has an account of the musician Bārbad playing for Khusraw, an incident usually found later in the narrative. There is, however, some logic to the introduction of Bārbad at this moment, since he was the fourth boon foretold by Anūshīrvān in Khusraw's dream, after the lady, who is of course Shīrīn, and Shabdīz, who has been left in the royal stables, and the inheritance of the throne.

Khusraw honoured by his subjects (No. 8, Narsingh; fig. 7) shows a number of men offering gifts and paying homage to the young prince. Among them a musician in pale blue, who must be Bārbad, seemingly sponsored by the man behind him, performs the obeisance known as *taslīm*. Khusraw, benign and simply dressed, is seated in a delicate pavilion in a green landscape. The fresh colour seems to symbolize the youthful hope of a new reign; the rendering of the distance is characteristic of the work of Narsingh, with thin colour, plentiful use of blue, and mop-headed trees.

Bahram Chūbīn, a grandee of the kingdom, rises against Khusraw and obliges him to leave Madā'in. Riding Shabdīz, Khusraw makes for Armenia where at last he comes face to face with Shīrīn, who is out hunting. They gaze at each other so intently that tears start to their eyes. If Khusraw cannot move from before Shīrīn, Shabdīz is equally captivated by her mount, Gulgūn (Rose-coloured). Overcome with emotion, Khusraw and Shīrīn slide unconscious from their saddles, but, recovering, they spring back into them. As their followers gather round them, Shīrīn offers Khusraw hospitality.

The composition of *Khusraw and Shīrīn meet on the hunting field* (No. 9, Nānhā; fig. 8) is symmetrical about a vertical axis: hills framing the scene, a vista between them, and Khusraw and Shīrīn facing each other. It is a moment of stillness. Colour is carefully orchestrated. The misty green valley suggests the delicate beginning of love. Two bright points are Khusraw's red *jāma* and Shīrīn's yellow shawl, colours that were often attributed to hero and heroine in Persian painting. Details of feminine costume – head-veils, slippers and decorative black pompoms – are lovingly rendered to emphasize the beauty of Shīrīn's companions.

Mihīn Bānū installs Khusraw in a palace, but she warns Shīrīn that she should not give herself to him until he has married her, and Shīrīn swears she will not. The lovers spend some time in amusements. By day they play polo or hunt; at night, when perfumes are carried on the breeze, they drink wine, and listen to stories told by their attendants.

It is probably by an oversight that *Shīrīn entertains Khusraw* (No. 10, Farrukh Chela and Dhanrāj; fig. 9) is not shown as taking place at night. Though at this period a night scene would not have been shown as fully dark, it would usually have included tokens of night, such as a moon or candles. The picture is the work of two painters: Farrukh Chela is credited with the colouring, and Dhanrāj with completing the faces. This form

Fig.10 *Khusraw defeats Bahrām Chūbīn*, f.72a (No. 11, Manohar).

Fig. 11 *Farhād before Khusraw*, Walters Art Gallery, Baltimore, 613, f. 5a (No. 12, Sānvala).

of co-operation was much used in the Mughal studio about the early 1590s when historical works were being produced, apparently at some speed; about the mid-1590s, when Akbar's attention had turned to works of classical Persian literature and he required a more exquisite finish, it became usual for illustrations to be entrusted to a single painter. In the earlier phase it is sometimes found that three painters work on a picture – one for composition, one for colour, and one for faces. *Shīrīn entertains Khusraw*, however, must surely have been designed as well as painted by Farrukh Chela. With its round towers, paired columns, and the alarming extension above the river, it exhibits his liking for strange and fanciful architecture, a taste which seems to have been nourished by European prints, and which is well suited to evoke a palace in distant Armenia. Though the architecture owes much to the imagination, the water system within it must reflect Mughal practice. The cattle turn a shaft which is geared to a great wheel with jars on its rim; water is raised from the river and eventually delivered to raised channels which intersect at right-angles forming a *chahārbāgh* or *chārbāgh*, a four-part garden. The flowers in the garden are chiefly crocuses, probably chosen to recall that Armenia is mountainous.

On a night in Spring, when Khusraw has urged Shīrīn to enjoy the sweetness of love and she has contrived to parry his advances, the prince falls asleep with his hand twined in her hair. Waking in the morning, Khusraw seizes Shīrīn, but she resists him and tells him that she will not be his until he has regained his kingdom. Stung by this rebuke, Khusraw leaves and goes to Constantinople to seek assistance from the emperor of Rūm ('Rome', meaning Byzantium); he is well received, even to the point of being granted the hand of the emperor's daughter, Maryam, in marriage.

Supplied with a powerful army, Khusraw attacks Bahrām Chūbīn by night. A great battle is fought; bowstrings twang, sabres rattle, horses are bathed in blood as though decked with rubies, lances thick as a forest block the way to retreat, arrows slide under armour as a breeze under rose petals. Khusraw fights on elephant-back; at a propitious moment he attacks Bahrām and throws him at his elephant's feet. Bahrām is vanquished but escapes with his life to China.

In *Khusraw defeats Bahrām Chūbīn* (No. 11, Manohar; fig. 10) it is the elephant, rather than his rider, who is the hero. The Indian tradition of fine paintings of elephants can be traced back to the Buddhist wall paintings, datable to the fifth century, at Ajanta, while the sculptural tradition extends to the intaglio seals of the Indus valley civilisation of three and half millennia BC; elephant portraiture was to be a feature of Mughal painting in the seventeenth century. It is typical of the work of Manohar that the action seems arrested at a significant moment, and that the beauty of the scene outweighs the horror.

Khusraw, though victorious and enthroned for a second time at Madā'in, is not able to banish from his mind the memory of Shīrīn. Meanwhile, Shīrīn herself weeps for Khusraw; she visits Mihīn Bānū who counsels her to have patience. Shortly after this, the queen dies and Shīrīn succeeds to the throne of Armenia. The country flourishes under her rule, but, learning that Khusraw has promised Maryam that he will take no other wife, she finds that she is distracted from the affairs of her people. She therefore entrusts her country to one of her lords and rides Gulgūn towards Madā'in, accompanied by Shāpūr and a baggage train with horses, camels, cattle and sheep; she installs herself in the castle that had been made for her. Informed of the death of Bahrām, Khusraw

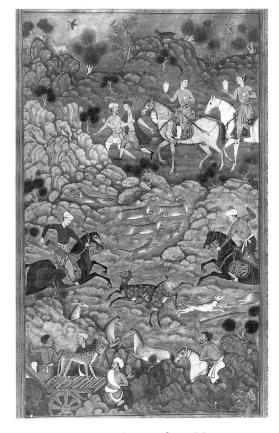

Fig.12 *Khusraw goes hunting*, f.82a (No. 13, Khvāja ʿAbd al-Ṣamad).

Fig.13 *Khusraw consults Buzurg Umīd about Shīrūya*, f.99b (No. 14, Maddū Chela).

finds himself saddened, but the approach of Shīrīn poses a more immediate problem. His solution, by the intermediary of Shāpūr, is to suggest that she should meet him in secret; on hearing this, Shīrīn vents her miserable rage on the messenger.

Shīrīn is accustomed to drink the milk of her flocks. However, these cannot be brought near her castle as it is surrounded by poisonous scrub. Shāpūr suggests that he should bring to her Farhād, an engineer well versed in geometry and highly skilled in carving rock, who had been his fellow student in China, Shāpūr learning to use the paintbrush and Farhād the chisel. Accordingly, the powerfully-built Farhād is brought to Shīrīn and, though she interviews him from behind the purdah-curtain, he at once falls in love with the sound of her voice: it is agreed that he shall carve a channel to bring the milk from the flocks. In a month the work is done; Shīrīn visits the channel and, with many apologies, offers Farhād in payment her jewelled earrings. Farhād lays these at her feet and retires to desert places so that people shall not hear him weeping for Shīrīn.

However, Khusraw is informed by one of his concubines of Farhād's love for Shīrīn and that he comes weekly to salute her castle. Khusraw's love for Shīrīn is inflamed, but with it comes jealousy. He discusses with his intimates what he should do about Farhād: can he put him to death? Khusraw is piqued since he considers Farhād a country bumpkin who is out of his mind; he is advised to offer Farhād money. Farhād is therefore brought before Khusraw. He is a mountainous figure but marked by grief; he does not look at

Fig.14 *Shīrīn kills herself at Khusraw's tomb*, f.102a (No. 15, Dharmdās).

Fig.15 *Niẓāmī gives his son to the son of the Shirvānshāh*, f.117a (No. 16, Khem Karan).

the king but seems, like a lion, to claw at the ground. Khusraw causes him to be seated and has gold piled before him; he then interrogates him, claiming possession of Shīrīn. At length Khusraw seeks to defeat Farhād by offering him the task of making a roadway through a mountain. Farhād will accept this challenge if the king will renounce Shīrīn: Khusraw thinks that he can safely accept this condition, since the feat is impossible; he indicates to Farhād the mountain now known as Bīsitūn. Overjoyed, Farhād sets to work. Before commencing he carves upon the mountain the figure of Shīrīn and that of Khusraw upon Shabdīz.

Farhād before Khusraw (No. 12, Sānvala; fig. 11) is the first of the pictures now in the Walters Art Gallery. Sānvala's carefully balanced composition focuses attention on Farhād, isolated between two groups of figures. His great size and strength are not apparent, but his relatively low social status is indicated by the plain brown *jāma*, and his craft by the mallet in his belt. He appears vulnerable in contrast to the rich princely trappings surrounding Khusraw.

Farhād works at the mountain by day and in the evening he covers the foot of the figure of Shīrīn with kisses and he laments. One day Shīrīn visits him, bringing a cup to milk to refresh him; when her horse is too tired to carry her home, Farhād carries Shīrīn upon her horse to her castle. Khusraw's informers tell him that Shīrīn has visited Farhād and also that the way through the mountain will be accomplished. On the advice of his confidants, Khusraw sends to Farhād a man who gives him false news of the death of Shīrīn. Farhād falls from the mountain and dies.

Shortly afterwards Maryam dies, but Khusraw then proposes marriage to another lady, Shakar (Sugar) of Isfahan. Shīrīn laments her loneliness and prays God for aid: in consequence of her prayer, Khusraw is moved to go hunting. With a brilliant retinue, princes at his stirrup, horses and elephants, attendants scattering rosewater, the crown of the great king Kay Qubād on his head, and the banner of the national hero Kāva the blacksmith above him, Khusraw approaches Shīrīn's castle.

Khusraw goes hunting (No. 13, Khvāja ʿAbd al-Ṣamad; fig. 12) is the work of a painter of Persian Muslim origin; his title *khvāja* may indicate either noble descent or mastery of painting. ʿAbd al-Ṣamad had joined Akbar's father, Humāyūn, in Kabul in 1549, and had then served Akbar, both as a painter and adminstrator; by 1595 he would have been of advanced years. A subject descended from ancient Persian tradition, his hunting scene is not a very specific illustration to the narrative, and we may speculate that it had been intended that the elderly master should depict the following episode, Khusraw before Shīrīn's castle, also of long Persian tradition. Though his style is classically Persian in conception, ʿAbd al-Ṣamad adopted Mughal techniques of modelling as they evolved.

When Khusraw presents himself at her castle, Shīrīn will not admit him but comes out to speak with him: she swears never to be his unless he will marry her. Khusraw returns to his camp, where Shāpūr attempts to cheer him. Full of regret, Shīrīn saddles Gulgūn and rides into the night after Khusraw. At Khusraw's camp she is recognized by Shāpūr, who agrees to hide her in a tent. Meanwhile, Khusraw has dreamed he held a torch, which Shāpūr interprets to mean he will attain his love. Khusraw orders an entertainment in his great tent; Bārbad plays his lute, then another musician, the harpist Nigīsā, secretly prompted by Shīrīn, sings of her love. The musicians continue to interpret the lovers' dialogue until Khusraw hears Shīrīn cry out in her tent. As he speaks to Shāpūr, she leaves her concealment; she permits Khusraw to kiss her, and he promises to marry her. Shīrīn is carried to her castle on a golden litter; then on an auspicious day, she is brought to Madā'in with great pomp, and the wedding is celebrated. Wives are also given to Shāpūr, Nigīsā, Bārbad and Buzurg Umīd, and Armenia is entrusted to Shāpūr. Khusraw is joyful and lives a life of pleasure for a time, but as he begins to age he grows sad. Shīrīn urges that he should take more interest in justice and learning, and Khusraw questions Buzurg Umīd on natural science and the meaning of life, including the role of the Prophet Muḥammad.

Khusraw has a son by Maryam, named Shīrūya, who has an evil disposition, an aspect of which is an incestuous desire for Shīrīn. Khusraw is troubled by his son's infatuation, and foresees that it will cause disaster. He discusses the youth with Buzurg Umīd, who can offer him no reassurance.

The raised finger of the king in *Khusraw consults Buzurg Umīd about Shīrūya* (No. 14, Maddū Chela; fig. 13) implies that he is asking for a point to be elucidated. The elder, bowing figure must surely be Buzurg Umīd; the youth in a golden surcoat, about to perform *taslīm*, seems to be Shīrūya, who properly should not be present in this scene. The odd composition with the action confined by a wall suggests a hidden tension: as in No. 5, it may be that the painter is wary of appearing to comment on the relations of royal fathers and sons.

When Khusraw retires to pursue a religious life at a fire-temple, Shīrūya hastens to ascend the throne. Shīrūya then confines Khusraw to a lonely place; Shīrīn, his only companion, endeavours to comfort him. One black night Khusraw falls asleep as Shīrīn chafes his chained legs, and then she too sleeps. Shīrūya enters and stabs Khusraw; as he bleeds to death, Khusraw is tormented by thirst, but he does not wake Shīrīn. In the morning Shīrīn lifts the coverlet and finds Khusraw lying in a sea of blood. She weeps and then prepares his body for burial. Shīrūya sends Shīrīn an invitation to share his power; she lulls him into confident expectation as she distributes Khusraw's clothes to the poor. Next morning she lays Khusraw in a coffin of aloe-wood and accompanies it to the tomb. She is dressed in rich jewels and silks of yellow and red; Shīrūya concludes that she loves him, as she dances among the weeping attendants. Shīrīn enters the tomb and shuts out the crowd. She uncovers Khusraw's wound and stabs herself in the same place; her blood warms his body as she clasps her wound to his. She cries out so that those outside shall know that she is united body and soul to Khusraw. The great ones of the court applaud what she has done and they shut the door of the tomb upon the royal couple.

Shīrīn kills herself at Khusraw's tomb (No. 15, Dharmdās; fig. 14) does not follow the text closely, since Khusraw's body is not shown, but it presents a powerful picture of how the scene might have appeared in a Mughal context. The walled garden-court indicates the royal privacy, which courtiers have just invaded. Shīrīn's posture is eloquent of her grief and devotion.

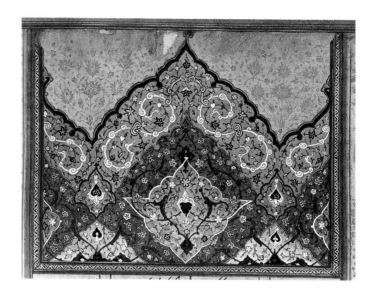

Laylā va Majnūn

Niẓāmī tells us that he has written his version of this story at the behest of Akhistān ibn Manūchihr, the Shirvānshāh. Urged by his son Muḥammad, Niẓāmī has accepted the task, and he gives his son into the service of the son of the Shirvānshāh.

It is unusual for the introductory matter of a romance to receive an illustration, but *Niẓāmī gives his son to the son of the Shirvānshāh* (No. 16, Khem Karan; fig. 15) is such a case. The situation evidently struck a chord in the Mughal period, and it may be that Akbar himself selected the subject for illustration because of some parallel to the affairs of his court. For example, the composition is close to that of an illustration in a copy of the *Akbarnāma* (The Story of Akbar), made about 1590 and now in the Victoria and Albert Museum, London, which shows Akbar in 1561 receiving ʿAbd al-Raḥīm, the son of Bayram Khān his former guardian. However that may be, the painter Khem Karan depicts the world he knows. Among those present is a plump, dark-skinned musician who was indeed a member of the Mughal court; he is known from a picture in the British Museum, and has been identified as ʿAlī Khān Karorī (fig. 16).

The remaining six illustrations in *Laylā va Majnūn* bears numbers in sequence from 17 to 22; however, they are out of narrative order. The confusion seems to date from the construction of the manuscript, since the numbers are supported by catchwords at the end of each folio. What this confusion means is not at present clear: it may be that it is in some way connected to the unusual choice of the first subject. The pictures will here be described in true narrative order: 20, 21, 18, 19, 17, 22.

A son is born to an Arab chieftain of the ʿĀmirī tribe and named Qays. He is sent to school, where he falls in love with Laylā, a beautiful girl from another tribe. While other pupils attend to their lessons, the couple think only of each other; but their love is soon observed, and tongues begin to wag. Qays becomes so maddened by love that he is nicknamed Majnūn – one possessed by a demonic *jinn*. Laylā is removed from contact with him, and Majnūn's madness increases. Sleepless and barefoot, ragged and singing of love, Majnūn runs about the desert, constantly returning to the place where Laylā's tribe dwells. Majnūn's father, Sayyid ʿĀmirī, requests Laylā's hand in marriage for his son, but Laylā's father will not countenance this. Sayyid ʿĀmirī, seeks out his son in the desert and pleads with him to return to a normal life; Majnūn replies that he cannot escape his fate.

The love between father and son in *Majnūn answers his father* (No. 20, Nand Gvāliyārī; fig. 17) is implied as they lean towards each other, but their eyes do not meet; between them stands a cypress tree which may represent Laylā. The father is dressed in sombre purple, over which floats a yellow scarf, hinting at the contrast between his emotion and his dignified exterior. The realistic treatment of the emaciated Majnūn suggests observation from life, but it also recalls ancient Indian sculptures of the fasting Buddha.

Majnūn goes home with his father, but soon returns to the desert. He is befriended by Nawfal, a bedouin, who determines to win Laylā for him by warfare. However, when battle is joined, Majnūn's sympathies are all with Laylā's tribe.

Fig. 16
ʿAlī Khān Karorī,
British Museum,
1989.8–18.1.

27

The battle of the tribes (No. 21, Nānhā; fig. 18) follows the tradition of illustrations in showing Majnūn as semi-naked, though in the narrative Nawfal has persuaded him to resume his clothes. Fragile in contrast to the heavily armed warriors, the figure of Majnūn is set off by a dark tree. Nānhā has made a gesture to the Arab setting with some camel-riders and examples of a turban worn with an end draped below the chin, but the Mughal world dominates, a musket and bucklers of wrapped and coiled wicker represented in careful detail.

Though Laylā's tribe is defeated, her father refuses to yield her up. Majnūn leaves Nawfal. Confirmed in his wandering life, he finds solace only in the company of the desert animals. He is again visited by his father, who tells him that he expects to die. Shortly after this, Majnūn encounters a hunter, who informs him of his father's death. Majnūn hurries to his father's tomb, falls upon it, and pours out his grief and remorse.

The wide vista and limpid colour of *Majnūn mourns his father's death* (No. 18, Manohar; fig. 19) convey a gently elegiac atmosphere rather than the acute grief of the text. By giving Majnūn a book, Manohar suggests that he is reading a prayer for the dead. Manohar was the son of the great painter Basāvan, and it may be that he introduces the wandering ascetic and his dog, subjects favoured by Basāvan, in tribute to his own father.

Salīm ʿĀmirī, Majnūn's maternal uncle, visits him and prevails upon him to accept clothing and food, though Majnūn says that he has no need of them. Majnūn asks after his mother, and Salīm ʿĀmirī brings her to visit him. She weeps at the sight he presents, runs her hands over his body, and begs him to return home. He replies that he cannot. Majnūn is soon to learn of his mother's death.

In *Majnūn visited by his mother and uncle* (No. 19, Sānvala; fig. 20) Sānvala plays on a number of contrasts. The rather plain and middle-aged mother, ordinary in terms of the world at large, who is anxiously trying to tempt her son to eat, finds herself in a strange situation – though paradoxically, in the field of the illustrated romance her ordinariness is the rarity. Meanwhile, the condition of Majnūn is contrasted with the abundant health of the surrounding animals – in particular with the power of tiger's neck under his skeletal arm – and his solitariness with the fact that they are in pairs. The notion of paired animals was probably prompted by the theme of Noah's Ark, which is found in a number of pictures at this period, in the wake of Jesuit missions.

During all this time Laylā has continued to love Majnūn. At one moment she has listened at a distance as Majnūn recited his poems in a palm-grove; at another he has managed to have himself brought to her tent in chains. Before the battle of the tribes she was betrothed to a man named Ibn Salām, and she was married to him after it, but she has refused to consummate the marriage. Now Ibn Salām dies. There follows a meeting of the lovers which is sometimes thought to have been interpolated into Niẓāmī's text: after mourning her husband for a year, Laylā sends a message to Majnūn by Zayd, who is himself a lover; Zayd brings Majnūn and his animals to Laylā's tent, where the couple swoon, while the animals form a protective ring around them; Zayd revives Majnūn with sprinkled rosewater; then Majnūn enters Laylā's tent, where the couple remain for a day and a night, after which Majnūn departs into the desert.

Laylā and Majnūn faint (No. 17, Farrukh Chela; fig. 21) is a climactic moment, amounting almost to a betrothal. The lovers lie symmetrically, the animals in a half circle

Fig. 17 *Majnūn answers his father*, f. 153b (No. 20, Nand Gvāliyārī).

29

Fig.18 *Battle of the tribes*, f.159a (No.21, Nānhā).

Fig.19 *Majnūn mourns his father's death*, f.132a (No.18, Manohar).

round them. The book in Majnūn's hand must be supposed to contain his love poems; the parrot on his arm is a symbol of desire. The stylized manner of Farrukh Chela emphasizes the strangeness of the scene; his elegant drawing and thin colour incline to a technique known as *nīm-qalam* (literally, 'half pen').

Laylā's health is undermined by sorrow and she dies of a fever. Accompanied by the animals, Majnūn comes to her burial place, where he spends days weeping. At last he dies embracing Laylā's tomb. The animals guard Majnūn's body, and people come to wonder at it. After a time a tomb is built for him beside that of Laylā.

The death of Majnūn on Laylā's grave (No.22, Sūr Gujarātī; fig.22) is at first sight rather like the picture of Majnūn at his father's grave, but it is much more bleak. There is no long background vista and signs of life are few. The usual animals are omitted, but a solitary jackal suggests a lonely place. A passer-by bites his finger as he contemplates the scene. Majnūn's face and body are very finely drawn.

(*Opposite page*) Fig.20 *Majnūn visited by his mother and uncle*, f.150b (No.19, Sānvala).

30

Fig.21 *Laylā and Majnūn faint*, f.123a (No. 17, Farrukh Chela).

Fig.22 *The death of Majnūn on Laylā's grave*, f.165b (No. 22, Sūr Gujarātī).

Haft Paykar

Yazdagird, king of Iran, has a son, who is named Bahrām. As none of the king's previous children has lived, the astrologers advise that it might be auspicious for Bahrām to be brought up among the Arabs of Yemen. Accordingly, Yazdagird entrusts the child to Nuᶜmān, the father of Munẕir. The child flourishes. Nuᶜmān builds for him a palace named Khavarnaq, and one day Bahrām enters a secret room within it and sees there the pictures of princesses of the Seven Regions of the world and of himself. On the death of Yazdagird, the great men of Iran do not summon Bahrām but place another on the throne. Learning of this, Bahrām advances with an army of Arabs; he proposes that the crown shall be given to him who can seize it from between two lions. The crown is thrown between two ravening lions, where it resembles the moon threatened by the dragons of the eclipse. Bahrām makes the first attempt: he dashes between the lions with a shout and takes up the crown; he kills the lions and seats himself upon the throne.

Bahrām Gūr takes the crown of Iran (No. 23, Mukund; fig. 23) offers two areas of interest. In the foreground, flanked by the carefully-drawn dead lions, Bahrām, the skirts of his gown tucked up for action and an expression of complete assurance on his face, places the jewelled cap of state over his turban. But attention is drawn away from this by the empty throne in the background, on its carpeted dais, framed by two awnings, and

32

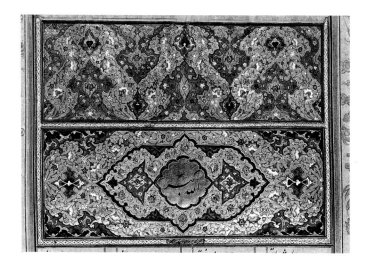

catching the eye by the white cloth over its bolster. By the urgent gestures of the courtiers the painter endeavours to signal that this is an exciting moment in the destiny of Iran, but the effect does not quite match the intention, perhaps because Mukund's heart is not in it.

Grateful for Bahrām's beneficent rule, his companions consider what might be done to make the king glad. Shīda, who had worked on Khavarnaq, offers to build a palace which will have seven pavilions: in each will be lodged a princess from one of the Seven Regions of the world; Bahrām will visit them in turn through the days of the week, wearing the colour appropriate to the planet associated with each day, and the princesses will entertain him with wine and stories. This manuscript illustrates three of the stories.

On Saturday, Bahrām visits the Black Pavilion, and enjoys the company of the Indian princess of the First Region. She tells him that she has known the former slavegirl of a king, who both alike wore black. The king told his slavegirl that a traveller, who wore black, had told him that in China was the City of the Stupefied, where all wear black. Consumed with curiosity, the king finds the city and with gold he prevails on an inhabitant to show him its secret. He is instructed to sit in a basket, and finds himself mysteriously raised to the top of a tower. On this vertiginous height the king begins to pray. Presently, a gigantic bird descends and preens itself, dislodging shells with pearls in them. The king sees that he has a chance of escape if he clings to the bird's leg. In this way he is carried to a beautiful garden, jewel-bright, full of flowers and scents and running waters. He wanders in the garden and then sees a light approaching. Many beautiful damsels come towards him, and they arrange a throne and carpets. At last appears their queen; she senses the presence of a stranger and sends one of her fairies to bring him forward. She makes the king welcome. For a month the queen dallies with him, without herself satisfying his desire, but providing him night by night with one of her companions. On the thirtieth night, seeming to accede to his wishes, she tells him to close his eyes for a moment. When he opens them he is again in the basket and he is taken down to the town. He has become one of those that wear black.

The king carried off by a bird (No. 24, Dharmdās; fig. 24) is a dazzling evocation of space. The great tower measures height, in contrast to the neat divisions of the agricultural landscape below. Dharmdās shows complete mastery of techniques derived from European manuscript painting. The notion of small figures to indicate distance is brilliantly applied. In effect, the distant landscape, normally an adjunct to the central action, has here taken over the whole, and for the first time the hero is himself a tiny distant figure. A feature of the distant landscape is that it may contain figures who are going about their business with no part in the main drama. This idea also has been incorporated, but here the apparently extraneous everyday world of the farmers and the wandering holy man is deliberately contrasted with the fabulous bird above. The latter is drawn according to the Chinese-influenced Persian tradition for the *Sīmurgh*, a bird of Persian mythology. The painter completes his picture by including, like a tragic chorus, the black-clad inhabitants of the City of the Stupefied, demonstrating by this his understanding of the story.

On Tuesday Bahrām visits the Red Pavilion, and the Slav princess of the Fourth Region tells him the following story. A king in Russia has a beautiful and learned daughter, who will not easily be persuaded to marry. She establishes herself in a castle, access to which is guarded by talismanic figures wielding sharp swords. A skilled painter, she makes a portrait of herself and inscribes over it the conditions to be met by the man who would win her hand: he must be personable; he must undo the power of the talismans; he must discover the door of the castle; and he must present himself before her father to answer questions she will pose. Many suitors are decapitated by the talismans. One day a prince who has gone hunting sees the portrait surrounded by a hundred heads; he is fascinated and day after day returns to contemplate the picture. At last he hears of a sage who can bind demonic forces, and takes advice from him on the management of the talismans. Dressed in red, the prince advances, destroying the talismans as he goes; at the wall he beats a drum and, attending to its resonance, he detects the position of the door. The test which the princess sets the prince is a conversation conducted by means of exchanges of pearls, a first pair symbolizing the brevity of life and a final pair the well-matched character of the couple. They are married and ever after he dresses in red.

The selection of *The princess paints a self-portrait* (No. 25, Jaganāth; fig. 25) is an indication of Akbar's high esteem for the art of painting. The princess works with a board on her knee, a maid before her holding a mirror, and her paints on what seems to be a lacquered tray. The life of the harem revolves around her. Painting was an activity open to Mughal princesses, and the Victoria and Albert Museum possesses a seventeenth-century picture attributed to a woman, Ṣaḥīfa Bānū. The fusion taking place under Akbar of elements from the European and Hindu traditions seems to be typified by a minute frieze running along the top of the foreground wall in which figures in sporting contests appear to draw on both European classical subjects and Hindu temple sculpture.

On Friday Bahrām visits the White Pavilion, where the princess of the Seventh Region tells him a story. Her mother once heard of a young man who had a very beautiful walled garden to which he would go every week to refresh himself. One day he finds the door shut against him and hears sounds of singing within. He makes a hole in the wall, climbs in, and is captured by two female guards who unbraid him. Learning that he is the rightful owner of the garden, the guards take him into a pavilion where, through a hole, he can see a group of ladies bathing in the garden pool; the guards offer to bring him her who pleases him most. The lady of his choice is brought to him and the door shut upon them. She returns his advances, but as his excitement grows to its climax, the room collapses about them, and the distressed couple run in different directions. The guards bring the couple together again, and the young man conducts the lady to a bower, but their amorous play is interrupted when a mouse gnaws through a vine and causes some gourds to fall with a resounding noise. A third encounter is attempted in a grotto, but this is frustrated when some foxes find it necessary to escape from a wolf. The guards lay hold of the lady and blame her for this third failure. However, the young man suddenly understands that the Divine Will has been preserving him from harm, and he proposes marriage to the lady. This concluded, his end is attained.

Fig. 23 *Bahrām Gūr takes the crown of Iran*, f.184b (No. 23, Mukund).

Fig.24 *The king carried off by a bird*, f.195a (No. 24, Dharmdās).

Fig.25 *The princess paints a self-portrait*, f.206a (No. 25, Jaganāth).

The man accompanied by two women at the bottom left of *The young man who sees ladies bathing in his garden* (No. 26, Sānvala; fig. 26) may be intended as the hero, accompanied by the guards, but if so, this ignores the fact that he should observe the scene from a pavilion; also, curiously, he is here transformed into an old man. The painter's attention is evidently mainly engaged by the women in the pool, who are seen behaving in a very natural way, clearly unconscious that they are being watched. Sānvala's confident portrayal of women in water may perhaps mean that, as a painter of Hindu origin, he was familiar with pictures of the Lord Krishna stealing the clothes of the *gopīs*, the cowherds' women, as they bathe in a river.

After Bahrām Gūr has visited all the princesses, a few events of his later life are recounted, followed by his final mysterious disappearance into a pit.

Fig. 26 *The young man who sees ladies bathing in his garden*, f. 220a (No. 26, Sānvala).

38

Iskandarnāma

The treatment of the story of Alexander the Great (356–23 BC) in Islamic literature diverges to a considerable extent from the historical fact, as it does in the literature of the Medieval West. The poet Firdawsī, writing *c.*1010, had seen Iskandar as the son of Dārāb of Iran (Darius II), by a daughter of Faylaqūs (Philip of Macedon), but Niẓāmī accepts him as the son of Faylaqūs. Iskandar is described, anachronistically, as ruler of Rūm, or Byzantium. Niẓāmī's romance is in two sections, *Sharafnāma* (The Book of Honour) which is loosely based on the events in Alexander's life, and *Iqbālnāma* (The Book of Progress) which concerns his prophethood and search for wisdom.

Sharafnāma

Niẓāmī asserts his belief that Iskandar was the son of Faylaqūs by a beautiful woman of his suite. Born in an auspicious hour, Iskandar is educated by a wise and learned man, Niqūmājus, the father of Arasṭū (Aristotle). When he succeeds to the throne of Rūm, Iskandar continues to pay tribute to Dārā (Darius III), and he rules with justice so that his fame spreads through the world. The people of Egypt appeal to him to deliver them from a ferocious black people, the Zangīs. Advised by Arasṭū, who has become his minister, Iskandar leaves Macedonia for Egypt. Iskandar leads his army into the desert towards the Zangīs. He sends an envoy, Ṭūṭiyā-nūsh, to the king of the Zangīs to ask him to desist from attacking Egypt. The Zangī king has Ṭūṭiyā-nūsh's throat cut and drinks his blood. In return, on the advice of Arasṭū, Iskandar pretends to eat a Zangī head, but substitutes for it that of a sheep. Battle follows and at length Iskandar defeats the Zangīs; he acquires much treasure, but he also reflects on how blame for the occurrence should be apportioned. He then enriches the Egyptians, founds the city of Alexandria, and returns to Rūm. When Iskandar sends a messenger with a portion of his booty to Dārā, the latter is filled with fear and envy and does not utter any word of thanks. This is reported to Iskandar who considers its implications. One day he sees two partridges fighting and takes an omen from it for his relations with Dārā: the bird he

39

Fig. 27–28 *Iskandar watches the invention of mirrors*, Walters Art Gallery, Baltimore, 613, f.17a (No. 30, Shīvdās), f.16b (No. 29, Nānhā).

chooses defeats the other, but soon after is killed by an eagle. Iskandar discusses with his counsellors the withholding of his tribute to Dārā and is advised that justice is on his side.

At this moment, when he has entered world affairs, Iskandar causes the first mirror to be made. First attempts with gold and silver fail but Rassām, a blacksmith, succeeds with iron; square and hexagonal shapes are found to distort, but a circular form is satisfactory. Before his nobles, Iskandar looks at his face in a round iron mirror and in delight kisses the back of it.

Conceived as a double-page, the two folios of *Iskandar watches the invention of mirrors* (No. 29, Nānhā – No. 30, Shīvdās; figs. 28–27) are now in the Walters Art Gallery. The mirror-making is clearly an important moment for Niẓāmī, since it interrupts the account of Iskandar's deteriorating relations with Dārā, and clearly it was important to Akbar also. The central idea appears to be that Iskandar has become visible in world affairs – that he has acquired a high profile. Probably to be associated with this are the concepts that the ruler should improve the world in a material way, typified by an invention; and that a great ruler is aware of what is happening beyond his immediate locality, suggested by the fact that the mirror is a device for seeing. Nānhā paints the righthand picture, showing a noble enthroned Iskandar. The larger turbans of some of the company indicate men of learning.

A messenger comes from Dārā to ask why Iskandar has withheld the usual tribute. Iskandar tells him that times have changed. When Dārā hears this he is furious and again sends his messenger to Iskandar, this time bearing a ball and polo-stick, and a measure of uncounted sesame seed. The messenger shows these to Iskandar, telling him that the first signifies that he is a child and the second shows the magnitude of the army that Dārā can bring against him. Iskandar, however, sees the stick as meaning that he will rule the world and the seed, which birds can devour, as showing that Dārā's army will be easy prey. Iskandar prepares his own army, but he also asks his counsellors whether it is right that he should oppose one of the Kayan line of kings of Iran. They assure him that it is, since Dārā is a tyrant; however, Iskandar should not shed the king's blood. Dārā and Iskandar exchange letters, but cannot come to terms. The two armies meet in the neighbourhood of Mosul and a great battle ensues (Gaugamela, 331 BC). Dārā fights like an enraged lion; Iskandar receives a wound. When the battle enters its second day, two of Dārā's officers come to Iskandar and offer to kill Dārā on the following day, if he will reward them. Iskandar agrees to this, though he scarcely believes that they will do the deed. The battle recommences, the armies mix and scatter over the plain; there comes a moment when none save the two officers is near Dārā, and they strike him. Informed of this, Iskandar repents of his ignoble agreement; he goes to Dārā and, supporting his head, he laments. Before he dies, Dārā pardons Iskandar; he asks him to punish his murderers, and, adjuring him to continue the line of the Kayan kings, he offers him his daughter Rawshanak.

Iskandar and the dying Dārā (No. 31, Dharmdās; fig. 29) is a subject of drama and pathos, and it is probably for this reason that it was allocated to Dharmdās, who had painted the death of Shīrīn. The subject was much favoured in the manuscripts of Iran and Dharmdās makes eloquent use of traditional poses for Iskandar and Dārā. This group is balanced, on the left, by the treacherous officers held prisoner.

Iskandar raises a domed tomb over Dārā. He has won the rulership of the world, and with it crown and throne and a great treasure. He makes gifts to rich and poor, and executes the murderers; he summons the great ones of the kingdom to him and they acknowledge his rule. Iskandar forbids the Zoroastrian religion and commends to the people the worship of the True God; he departs from Mosul and destroys the fire-temples of Azerbaijan. He moves to Isfahan and makes a formal approach to Rawshanak's mother for her daughter's hand. When this is accepted, he marries Rawshanak, naming Iran as her dowry. Then he ascends the Kayan throne at Istakhr (Persepolis).

As Stuart Cary Welch has noted, the form taken by the crown of Iran in *Iskandar assumes the crown of Iran* (No. 32, Bem Gujarātī; fig. 30) is the headdress – split-brimmed cap and turban swathe – associated with Akbar's father Humāyūn. Clearly, the intention is to associate the Mughal house with the legitimate rule and liberality of Iskandar.

Iskandar decides on further campaigning, though it is not solely lust for conquest that moves him, but also the desire to promote the welfare of mankind. For safety he sends Rawshanak with his minister to Rūm. First Iskandar travels westwards to Arabia and performs the rites of pilgrimage at the Kaʿba (in Mecca). Returned to Isfahan, he receives a message which tells him that Armenia is in the hands of Davālī, a fire-worshipper. Iskandar makes his victorious way through Armenia and Abkhazia; then he determines to visit Nūshāba, the queen of Bardaʿ.

Iskandar pitches camp near Bardaʿ and presents himself to Nūshāba in the guise of his own envoy. However, his bold behaviour does not match this persona, and Nūshāba guesses that he is himself Iskandar. She invites him to sit with her upon the throne and tells him that she knows he is Iskandar. He denies his identity, until Nūshāba orders an attendant to bring a silken scroll which contains portraits of the kings of the world, and shows him his own picture. Nūshāba then descends from her throne and orders her women to prepare a feast for Iskandar, but first she has him offered an inedible banquet of dishes filled with jewels, to show the futility of an attachment to such stones. Iskandar makes a peace treaty with Nūshāba and returns to his camp. On the following day, Nūshāba rides out brilliantly dressed to Iskandar's camp. He seats her upon a throne and entertains her with a banquet and music and wine until dawn; at this autumnal feast a great fire is kindled. In the Spring Iskandar holds another great feast for Nūshāba; rich foods and scents, wine and the sound of the harp render him almost insensible as he embraces the narrow-eyed beauty. When half the day has passed he presents Nūshāba and her attendants with robes of honour and other gifts.

Iskandar and Nūshāba entertained (No. 33, Bhūra; fig. 31) is perhaps the least satisfactory illustration in the manuscript, evoking neither the clearly defined incidents of the early part of the Nūshāba story, nor the subsequent feasts, where the very vagueness of the description contributes to the heady atmosphere.

Iskandar gathers the commanders of his army together and tells them what he intends to do: he purposes to travel the world from end to end, to subdue it, and to seek out those who are happy in the hope of acquiring the secret of their happiness. The commanders agree to follow him.

Iskandar proceeds on his way, and wherever he hears of a hermit he visits him to ask for his blessing. This practice begins to annoy his commanders. It happens, however,

Fig.29 *Iskandar and the dying Dārā*, Walters Art Gallery, Baltimore, 613, f.26b (No. 31, Dharmdās).

Fig.30 *Iskandar assumes the crown of Iran*, Walters Art Gallery, Baltimore, 613, f.34a (No. 32, Bem Gujarātī).

Fig.31 *Iskandar and Nūshāba
entertained*, f.244b (No. 33, Bhūra).

that the army finds its way blocked by the fortress of Darband, which is occupied by robbers, and that it is unable to take it by force. Iskandar inquires whether there might be a hermit living in the vicinity and, learning that there is, he visits him to ask for help. With a powerful exhalation the sage reduces the fortress, and Iskandar returns to his camp to find the army commanders ready to apologize to him.

Iskandar is welcomed at the fortress of Sarīr. He sits for a moment on the throne of Kay Khusrau, a former king of the Kayan line, and drinks from his world-revealing cup of turquoise – the archetype of the mirror made for himself. Then he is guided to the cavern into which Kay Khusrau disappeared.

From there Iskandar travels eastwards, by way of Rayy, Nishapur, Marv, Balkh and Ghur, to the borders of Hindustan. He sends a letter to the Indian Kayd (ruler), Fūr

Fig.32 *Iskandar shown gifts from the Kayd*, f.254a (No. 34, Dharmdās).

(Porus) of Kannauj, requiring his submission. The Kayd realizes that he cannot resist Iskandar, and he sends him four incomparable gifts – his daughter, a ruby cup, a philosopher and a physician – together with his own envoy. The Indian envoy is received in Iskandar's tent and bows to the ground.

Only one figure in *Iskandar shown gifts from the Kayd* (No. 34, Dharmdās; fig. 32) seems to be represented as Indian, with darker skin, a different form of turban and a transparent *jāma*; he is perhaps the physician. The kneeling turbaned figure is probably the philosopher. The princess and the ruby cup are not shown. Instead, there is an array of the sort of gift more usually seen in the Mughal court: ornate weapons and vessels of gold.

Iskandar then turns his attention to effecting the submission of China and enters into

correspondence with the Khāqān of Chīn. The Khāqān visits Iskandar and submits to him. While he is Iskandar's guest he arranges a contest between the wall-painters of Rūm and those of Chīn. Each side is to paint a picture in an alcove. The painters of Chīn polish their wall so that it reflects the work of the painters of Rūm opposite to it: the Rūmīs are judged the better painters and the Chīnīs the better polishers.

At this point Niẓāmī interpolates a story of Mānī, founder of Manichaeism, an offshoot of Zoroastrianism, who was born in Seleucia-Ctesiphon, lived *c*.215–75, and who was seen traditionally as a painter, presumably on the basis of surviving illustrated copies of the Manichaean scriptures. Mānī sets out from Iran to work amongst the Chinese, but to hinder his coming they put in his way a pool of crystal which has been painted with wavelets to look like water. Approaching this and feeling thirsty, Mānī brings his flask to the water, and it breaks on the stone. Mānī takes out his brush and on the pool he draws a dead dog, and in it writhing worms to fill any thirsty traveller with horror. Impressed by this, the Chinese incline to Mānī's teaching.

Mānī paints a dead dog (No. 35, Sūr Gujarātī; figs. 33 and 34) must have been chosen for illustration because it provides an opportunity to show a painter at work: thus it

(*Opposite page*) Fig.33 *Mānī paints a dead dog*, f.262b (No. 35, Sūr Gujarātī).

(*Right*) Fig.34 *Mānī paints a dead dog* (detail), f.262b (No. 35, Sūr Gujarātī).

demonstrates the high esteem in which Akbar held his painters. Sūr Gujarātī is a painter who seems to have had a particular liking for showing people in the context of their work, as he was allocated this type of subject matter in several manuscripts. The pigments used in the Mughal studio were mainly mineral, with some animal and vegetable additions, in a medium of gum and water.

The Khāqān feasts Iskandar and presents him with a horse, a hawk and a beautiful slavegirl. Then Iskandar turns his face towards Rūm, but his former adversary Davālī brings him news that the army of the Rūs (Russians) has invaded Abkhazia and Barda^c, and taken Nūshāba captive, laid waste the country and burnt villages: they are robbers like wolves and lions, and will soon threaten Khurasan and Rūm. Iskandar resolves to punish the Russians. He passes through the desert of Khwarazm until he comes to the Qipchāq steppe, where the army of Rūm encounter beautiful women who are not in the habit of veiling themselves. Iskandar fears the effect that these may have upon his soldiers, who have been on campaign for so long. He suggests to the leaders of the Qipchāqs that the custom should be changed; they represent to him that in this matter it is the eye of the beholder rather than the face of the beheld which is at fault. Gaining nothing from them, Iskandar consults one of his wise counsellors, and the latter says that he will sculpt a talisman to be set up in the desert which will cause all the women to veil themselves. Accordingly, it is made, a woman in black stone with a veil of white marble, and the Qipchāq women change their ways. The statue remains in the desert and is to become an object of veneration.

Niẓāmī's account of this incident is probably to be related to the fact that his first wife was a Qipchāq; he would have known at firsthand the freer ways of the women, and possibly also have heard of some monument which he interprets as the talisman. The reason for the choice of *The talisman that causes the Qipchāq women to veil themselves* (No. 36, Mukund; fig. 35) for illustraton in Akbar's copy is probably less an interest on his part in the promotion of the veil, than in an example of the power exerted by an object of art. Mukund duly renders the statue as though it were carved in black schist. It is possible that his composition may owe something to a version of a Christian subject, *The women at the sepulchre* or *The raising of Lazarus*, the statue taking the place of the angel or of the wrapped body.

The armies of Rūm and Rūs meet and there is battle for five days. On the sixth day the Rūs deploy a monstrous being of terrible strength; clothed in a sheepskin and with fettered leg, it wreaks destruction with an iron crook. This being is described to Iskandar: it lives in the mountains, has a red face, and blue eyes, and a horn like that of a rhinoceros, which it presses into the branch of a tree so that it can hang sleeping at night. On the seventh day of battle the Russian giant tears the trunk from an elephant. Iskandar is disconcerted, but his wise counsellor advises him that, though a sword will not avail against the giant, he can be tamed with a lasso. Iskandar catches him in this way and the monster submits.

The champion of Rūs wounds an elephant (No. 37, Farrukh Chela; fig. 36) shows a giant with flaming blue eyes, tusks which mimic the line of moustache, and horns ornamented with golden bands and bells, but wearing conventional clothing. The horrific depiction of the wounded elephant follows the manner of the *Ḥamzanāma* (The Epic of Ḥamza), produced for Akbar in the 1560s and 1570s. A striking vignette of distant landscape in the upper left shows blue rain-clouds breaking over mountains; it is perhaps an interpretation of the climate of Russia by a painter who is working from his knowledge of the monsoon.

Iskandar rests and surveys a rich booty of gold and silver and precious furs, for which he thanks God; then he has Nūshāba freed and gives her in marriage to Davālī. After this, Iskandar dallies for a time with the slavegirl given him by the Khāqān of Chīn, who has taken part in the battle and was captured by the Russian champion.

One day, after he has offered prayer to God, Iskandar turns to wine and sociability. There is talk of the wonders of the world, and an old man tells him that under the North Pole is the Land of Darkness, where a spring, the Water of Life, confers protection on the life of those who drink it. Iskandar sets out to find the Water of Life; as the way is difficult, he selects a small band to accompany him.

Fig.35 *The talisman that causes the Qipchāq women to veil themselves,* f.266b (No. 36, Mukund).

Fig.36 *The champion of Rūs wounds an elephant*, f.273a (No. 37, Farrukh Chela).

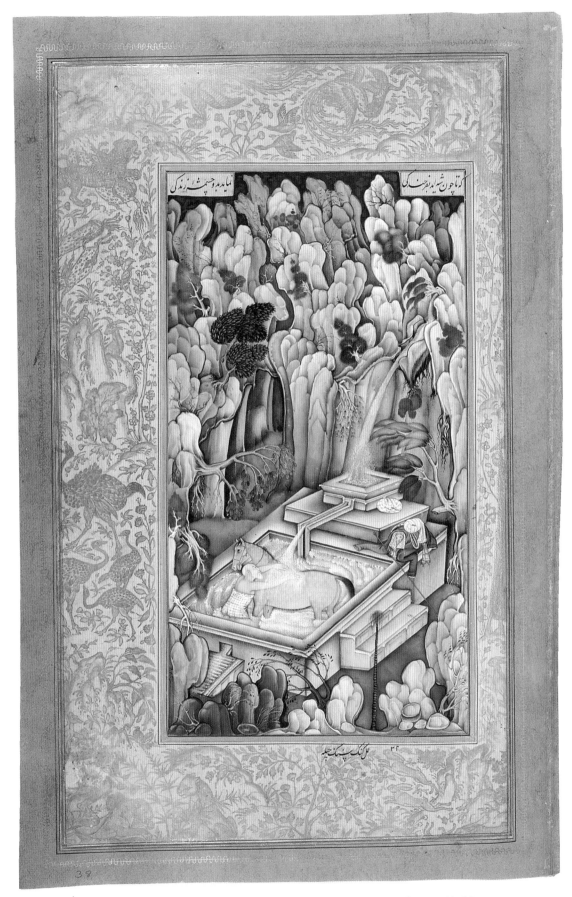

Fig.37 *Khiżr washes Iskandar's horse in the Water of Life*, f.281a (No. 38, Kanak Sing Chela).

The Prophet Khiżr is to go in front on Iskandar's grey horse, taking with him a jewel which will shine when it comes to the water. The jewel slips from Khiżr's hand and he discovers below him a spring of silver water issuing from the navel of the rock, or rather a spring of light in constant motion. Khiżr lays aside his clothes and bathes in the spring and drinks from it; he washes Iskandar's horse and waters it. As he contemplates the spring, thinking that he will soon be able to show it to Iskandar, it vanishes, and so he understands that Iskandar is not destined to find it.

The dark background and strange rock-forms of *Khiżr washes Iskandar's horse in the Water of Life* (No. 38, Kanak Sing Chela; fig. 37) express the mysterious, subterranean quality of the Land of Darkness. The Water of Life is shown jetting with great energy from the rock and through three levels of a Mughal water system. Kanak Sing Chela, following the text closely, shows in detail the clothes that Khiżr has taken off before washing the horse, so that a powerful contrast is created between the other-worldly and the mundane.

Resigned to the fact that it is not his destiny to find the Water of Life, Iskandar returns to the body of his army. By way of the land of Rūs, he returns to Rūm, where he is greeted with jubilation. He reposes for a while and deputes regents to his various lands. Iskandar now knows that the key to the door of happiness is found by way of learning and godly wisdom.

f.285b

Iqbālnāma

Iskandar spreads enlightenment and pursues learning, whether in the Greek or Persian languages. The Book of the Persian Kings and other works are translated for him; and a book of geography, a book on spiritual beings and a book on his travels are produced. He lets it be known that the wise are honoured at his court, and he holds artists in the highest esteem. Iskandar himself, however, leads a simple life and spends much time in prayer. He is always accompanied by soldiers, magicians, translators, wise men, ascetics or prophets.

One day a slavegirl in whom Iskandar takes delight is stricken with a fever for which no remedy can be found. Anxious for her life, Iskandar wanders restlessly to the palace

54

roof. From there he sees an old shepherd who strolls forward, giving his attention now to a plant, now to his sheep. Pleased by his apparent intelligence, Iskandar has him brought to the roof and asks him to entertain him. The shepherd asks Iskandar what is troubling him and then tells him a story. When he was young, the shepherd says, he served a prince of Marv who loved a beautiful concubine who fell sick of a fever and whose life was despaired of. The prince went into the nearby Desert of Death, with the intention of killing himself, but a friend followed after him, caught him, blindfolded and imprisoned him. The friend found a remedy for the girl's fever. He then arranged a feast, to which he brought both the concubine and also the prince, still blindfolded. When the blindfold was removed the prince felt that he had been transported from Hell to Heaven. Iskandar is calmed and shortly after receives news that his girl has been cured; he rewards the shepherd. Such stories, says Niẓāmī, are known to the pure in heart and understood by them.

The fund of wisdom at Iskandar's court proves to be of benefit to Māriya, a Copt, whose father was a prince of Syria. Forced from her inheritance by her enemies, she comes to the ruler of the world to ask for justice but, encountering his learned minister, she instead becomes absorbed in study. The minister, Arasṭū, instructs her and, when she has become very learned, he teaches her alchemy so that she may make gold and thus be able to regain her lands. This achieved, Māriya's ability becomes known to certain learned but indigent men and they desire the knowledge of the preparation of her alchemical elixir. Māriya receives them at an elegant pavilion, dressed in bridal finery,

Fig.38 *Māriya and the would-be alchemists*, f.294a (No. 39, Sānvala).

Fig.39 *Aflāṭūn charms the animals*, f.298a (No. 40, Maddū Khāna-zād).

her face veiled in black silk, and pearls in her black hair, two locks of which are wound crosswise into the pearls. She tells the seekers to look at the locks over her eyebrows and the rising sun of her brow: since she herself represents the elixir, the secret is hidden there. The seekers fail to understand this. On the following day, they return and Māriya mounts to the upper floor of her pavilion. She speaks to them of herbs, but her meaning is concealed from those without knowledge, for if the elixir comes of a plant, it is the reed-pen.

The association between black and white – ink and paper – and hence between writing and the learning which is within Māriya's mind is not taken up in *Māriya and the would-be alchemists* (No. 39, Sānvala; fig. 38), but earlier treatments of the subject do not show it either. Instead we have a graceful picture of a princess addressing a group of men from her pavilion. The detailed treatment of the architecture and water-raising mechanism lend it a very realistic air. There is perhaps a recollection of a picture in the *Hamzanāma* which features another exceptional woman in the upper floor of a pavilion, *Mihrdukht shoots at the ring*.

One day when Iskandar is on his throne with the philosophers ranged before him, one expounding science, another theology, another mathematics, and another literature, Arasṭū caps all their discourses and vaunts himself as the fount of all knowledge. As he has the support of Iskandar all add their voices to his praise. This enrages Aflāṭūn (Plato), who was the true originator of all branches of learning, and he withdraws and considers how he may discover hidden melodies. He enters into a barrel to learn the music of the seven spheres. Then he stretches leather over a gourd and, perfuming the gazelle-skin with musk, he sets strings to them and constructs an organ which produces the correct tones. This he plays, imitating the sounds of all animals and men, so that the latter dance and sing and the former fall into sleep or awaken. Aflāṭūn thus creates a new music with melodies in harmony with every being so that when played they give any doctor or king a better understanding of his business. This organ he takes into the wilderness and plays. The wild and tame animals run to him and fall unconscious around him; then he plays another melody and they return to consciousness. News of this comes to Iskandar's palace, and Arasṭū is put to shame.

In *Aflāṭūn charms the animals* (No. 40, Maddū Khāna-zād; fig. 39) the brilliant portrayal of unconscious animals probably draws on the sight of game dead after the hunt, a scene which may have been familiar to Maddū from childhood, as his epithet shows that he was born in the royal household; amongst the known creatures he wittily introduces the fabulous *Sīmurgh*. The organ, which would be portable and follows a European pattern, may have been copied from a real example – though it seems to lack bellows. It is shown as though decorated with a collage of tinted drawings: a bust of a man with a European hat; an artist drawing a European; the Nativity; and Majnūn in the desert.

Iskander has distributed such gifts that there is no more poverty in his land. One day he sits on his throne discoursing on justice and religion when he is moved to withdraw into his private apartment for further discussion. He selects to accompany him the seven wisest philosophers: Arasṭū, Vālīs (Thales), Balīnās (Apollonius), Suqrāṭ (Sokrates), Farfūriyūs (Porphyrius), Hirmis (Hermes), and Aflāṭūn. Iskandar desires to know how the world came into being. He hears the opinion of his seven philosophers, and then

Fig.40 *Iskandar and the seven philosophers*, f.305a
(No. 41, Nānhā).

Fig.41 *Iskandar crossing the 'Race of Death'*, f.312b
(No. 42, Bem Gujarātī).

expresses his conviction that the world is the work of a Creator, whose ways are beyond human understanding.

The composition of *Iskandar and the seven philosophers* (No. 41, Nānhā; fig. 40) follows the same lines as Nānhā's portion of *Iskandar watches the invention of mirrors* and, as in that, pointing fingers direct attention from the centre and towards the left. On the left of the present picture is a carpeted gallery containing the philosophers, carefully differentiated but tightly packed together, so that they seem to be treated with a touch of satire. On a book held by one of the philosophers Nānhā has contrived to sign his name followed by an additional letter *nūn* (n). The watching attendants on the right hold the royal weapons in bags.

God's messenger, the angel Surūsh, announces to Iskandar that he has attained prophethood: he is to travel the world exhorting mankind to turn from evil ways to good. Iskandar departs, leaving his revenues to his son. With selected troops and many baggage animals, he journeys through many lands. He approaches a terrible place which is covered with blue, red, yellow and black rocks. These have the property that anyone beholding them is seized with such uncontrollable laughter that he dies; however, very small rocks are not dangerous. The place is called the 'Race of Death'. Scouts are sent

Fig. 42–43 *The priestess of Kandahar beseeches Iskandar to spare an idol*, f. 318a (No. 44, Mukund), f. 317b (No. 43, La‘l).

out to assess the situation and some indeed die. Iskandar orders his people to blindfold their eyes, wrap the rocks carefully and load them on their horses and pass on quickly. Further on Iskandar has the rocks built into a monument; the exterior is rendered innocuous with a covering of plaster, but the cloth covering eventually wears away from the interior, which reverts to deadliness.

Iskandar crossing the 'Race of Death' (No. 42, Bem Gujarāti; fig. 41) omits the blindfolds, but the coloured stones can be seen through their wrappers. The powerful horses and camels and detailed treatment of baggage suggest a realistic picture of the Mughal army on the march.

Iskandar makes a second visit to India, and after suffering severe heat he comes to the beautiful city of Kandahar. He finds a temple where many maidens venerate an enormous golden image of the Buddha that has two glittering jewels for eyes. He orders the image to be reduced to its component gold and jewels. A beautiful damsel comes forward and begs him to hear the story of the image. In former times when the dome of the temple had been half fallen-in, two birds had appeared carrying in their beaks jewels, which they had deposited there. To prevent strife over the ownership of these, the people had made an image of gold and set in it the jewels, which were evidently a gift from heaven. Hearing this, Iskandar spares the image.

As a double-page and the last illustration, *the priestess of Kandahar beseeches Iskandar to spare an idol* (No. 43, La⁽l – No. 44, Mukund; figs. 43–42), was clearly deemed an important subject. The intention must surely be to associate Akbar with Iskandar's liberal act in sparing the idol. On one level, this is a topical reference, as the Mughals had taken Kandahar from the Safavids of Iran without bloodshed in the April of 1595. More generally, there is probably an allusion to Akbar's tolerant religious policies. As early as 1562, Akbar had found it politic to marry a Rajput princess, the daughter of Rājā Bihārī Mall of Amber, and in 1564 he had abolished the poll-tax on his Hindu subjects. His interest in comparative religion had developed, and in 1582 he had established a syncretistic faith of his own, the *Dīn-i ilāhī* (Divine Faith). A figure whose presence supports the contention that the picture intends contemporary references is the court recorder, notebook in hand. Later to be found in illustrations of events in recent Mughal history, such figures are not characteristic of illustrations to classical literature. In the lefthand picture, the image is more Hindu than Buddhist in character, as might be expected from Akbar's painters drawing on their own experience.

Iskandar visits the Khāqān of Chīn, whom he converts to true religion. Then Iskandar explores the wonders of the sea. Returned to dry land, he journeys to the north and builds a wall to keep out a savage people of horrible appearance called the Ya'jūj (the biblical Gog and Magog).

In the season of Autumn, Iskandar hears a voice telling him to return to Rūm; he dies as he approaches it. His mother is informed of his death, as is his son, who renounces the throne. Nizāmī concludes the poem by describing the end of the life of each of the philosophers – to which the record of his own death is appended.

Fig.44 Colophon to
Khusraw va Shīrīn,
f.109b.

Fig.45 Colophon to
Laylā va Majnūn,
f.168a.

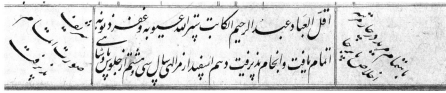

Fig.46 Colophon to
Sharafnāma, f.284b.

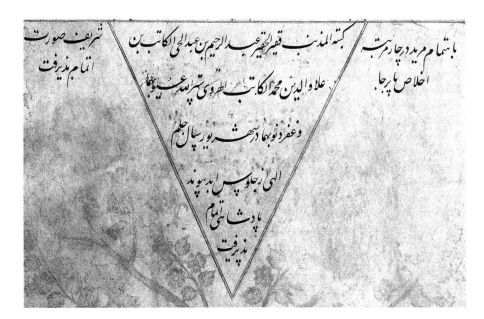

Fig. 47 Final colophon, f. 325b.

64

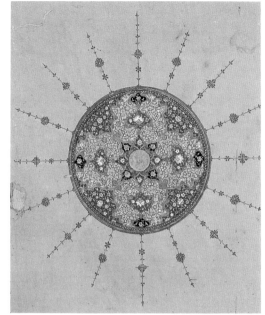

Fig.48 *Shamsa*, f.32a.

Fig.49 *Shamsa*, f.31b.

Colophon dates and scribe

The manuscript contains four dated colophons which show that the copying of the text took more than two years. As is often the case with Akbar's manuscripts, the dates are not recorded by the Muslim calendar, but according to the *ilāhī* era, instituted by Akbar in 1584 as an aspect of his Divine Faith – but perhaps not uninfluenced by Pope Gregory XIII's calendar reform of 1582. The *ilāhī* calendar follows the Zoroastrian solar pattern with months of Persian name and a New Year in March; the years are counted from Akbar's accession, 1556 being year 1.

Khusraw va Shīrīn was completed on 20 Mihr in the 38th year/12 October, 1593 (Gregorian or New Style calendar); Akbar's name and titles are here picked out in gold (fig.44. f.109b). *Laylā va Majnūn* was completed on 10 Isfandārmuz in the 38th year/1st March, 1594 (fig.45, f.168a). The *Sharafnāma* was completed in Shahrīvar in the 40th year/August–September, 1595 (fig.46, f.284b). The final colophon after the *Iqbālnāma* is dated 24 Aẕar (*sic*) in the 40th year/14 December, 1595 (fig.47, f.325b).

The colophons, including two undated ones, contain the name of the scribe (*kātib*) ʿAbd al-Raḥīm. The fullest version of his signature, ʿAbd al-Raḥīm al-kātib ibn ʿAbd al-Hayy al-kātib ibn ʿAlāʾ al-Dīn Muḥammad al-kātib al-Haravī, shows that his father and grandfather had also been scribes, and that the latter came from Herat, in what is now Afghanistan. ʿAbd al-Raḥīm was among the most celebrated calligraphers of Akbar's day, and his *nastaʿlīq* script is both elegant and vital. When the *Khamsa* manuscript passed to Akbar's son and successor, Jahāngīr, a portrait of ʿAbd al-Raḥīm was added below the final colophon, together with a self-portrait of the painter who executed it, Dawlat (fig.47). The open book in front of the scribe gives his name with the title ʿ*Anbarīn-qalam* (Pen of Ambergris), implying that his black script is so beautiful as to seem perfumed.

The paper on which he writes appears to have carried the same message. The inscription on the dado behind the two figures announces that Jahāngīr ordered this picture to be added; it includes a date of the Muslim era in figures which, though damaged, has been published by J. P. Losty as 102(-?), equivalent to a date between 1611 and 1620.

Painters

The senior painter, Khvāja ʿAbd al-Ṣamad, appears to be the sole Muslim. The names of Hindu painters working for Akbar sometimes present problems, since their spelling may vary, presumably as supervisors in the Mughal library sought to refine their transliteration into Persian characters; in addition, scholars have adopted various conventions to transliterate the results into Roman characters. In this manuscript the problems are exemplified by the question whether Mādhū (or probably better, Mādhav) of No. 6 should be identified with Maddū of Nos. 14 and 40. Maddū's name is accompanied by epithets: in No. 14, Chela, 'disciple or student', and in No. 40, Khāna-zād, 'born in the household', implying that his father had already been employed in the royal service. Manuscripts record the existence of a 'senior' and 'junior' Mādhū, presumably father and son, so it may be that No. 6 should be ascribed to the father and Nos. 14 and 40 to the son. Stylistic considerations, however, would tend to unite Nos. 6 and 40, with No. 14 as the singleton. Assuming that Mādhū and Maddū are two individuals, the Hindu painters of the original work are twenty in number. In alphabetical order, they are: Bem (sic) Gujarātī, Bhūra, Dhanrāj, Dharmdās, Farrukh Chela, Jaganāth, Kanak Sing (sic) Chela, Khem Karan, Laʿl, Maddū Chela, Mādhū, Manohar, Miskīna, Mukund, Nand Gvāliyārī, Nānhā, Narsingh, Sānvala, Shīvdās, and Sūr Gujarātī. To these must be added Dawlat.

The arts of the book

The non-illustrative illumination consists of headings to the different books (ʿunvān), ornamental rosettes (shamsa, 'sun'), and marginal decoration in a chinoiserie mode. The ʿunvāns to Khusraw va Shīrīn (f. 32b) and Haft Paykar (f. 169b) are signed by Khvāja Jān; the latter adds the title naqqāsh (illuminator) and the date 1004/1595–6. The work is done in a wide range of colours with prominent use of black; portions of goldwork are overlaid with a dimming pigment to create a contrast between matt and shining. A damaged portion of the first shamsa (fig. 51) has been restored. The marginal work is done in brush-gold, in a tradition derived from Iran, which in its turn had been much influenced by China. Fabulous creatures, such as sīmurghs, are joined by those of the Indian Subcontinent (fig. 50). Subheadings in the text are very plain, but the introduction of birds (f. 132b) suggests that the confusion in text order had been discovered. The lacquered covers, painted on prepared cardboard and varnished, have been reversed so that the pictorial outsides have changed places with the chinoiserie doublures; the central fields of all four faces appear to have been revarnished.

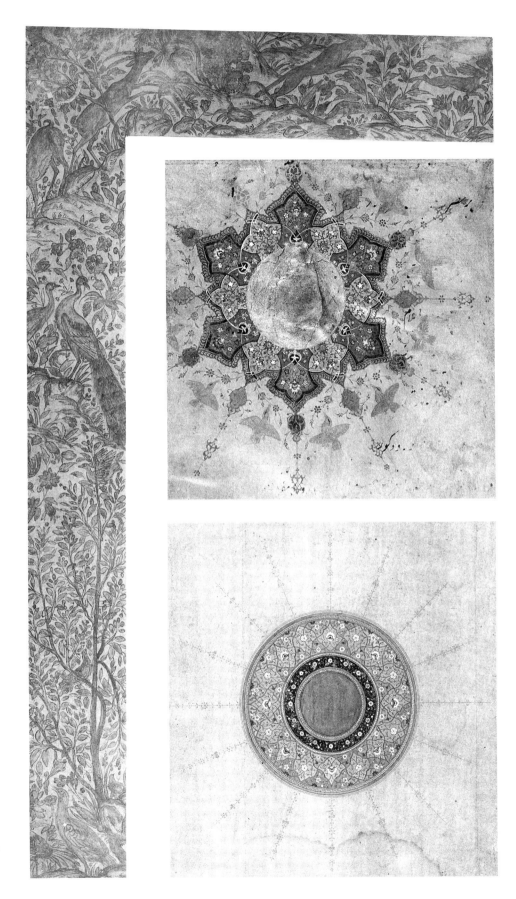

(*Right*) Fig.50
Marginal
decoration with
peacock, f.235a.

(*Far right, top*)
Fig.51
Shamsa, f.1a.

(*Far right, below*)
Fig.52
Shamsa, f.285a.

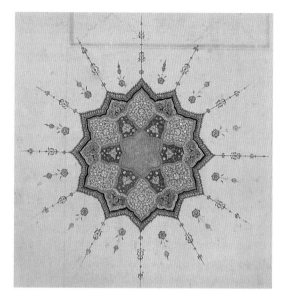

Fig.53 *Shamsa*, f.110a.

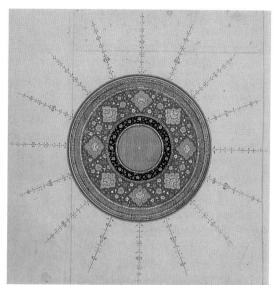

Fig.54 *Shamsa*, f.231a.

Fig.55 *Shamsa*, f.169a.

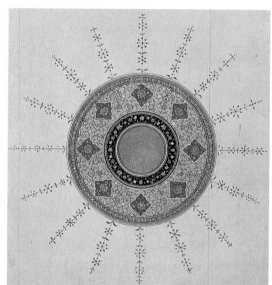

Fig.56 *Shamsa*, f.168b.

(*Opposite page*)

(*Top, left*) Fig.57 *Sīmurgh* attacks cloud-lion. Former doublure of front cover, now front cover.

(*Top, right*) Fig.58 Game-bag presented to enthroned ruler (Akbar?). Former front cover, now doublure of front cover.

(*Below, left*) Fig.59 Princely hunt. Former back cover, now doublure of back cover.

(*Below, right*) Fig.60 Lion attacks dragon. Former doublure of back cover, now back cover.

68

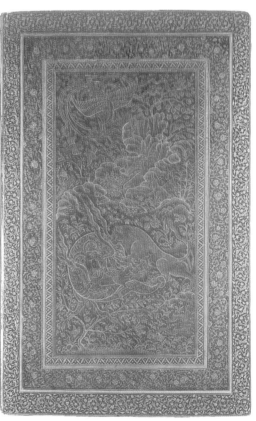

The meaning of the manuscript

The first dated colophon begins 'This noble book was brought to a conclusion and received its completion, commissioned for the treasury of books and august library, servants of His Majesty . . .'. The principal impression made by this formulation is ceremonious, even grandiloquent, nevertheless it contrives, in its seemingly loose syntax, to bring momentarily into view the library staff, who are not usually mentioned in such a context. A personage such as the director of the library must have been in charge of the production of the *Khamsa*. He would have proposed to Akbar, or received from him, the selection of subjects to be illustrated.

Kingship is an important topic. Subjects Nos. 1 and 2 are so widely used that their warning regarding kingly justice would carry no sting. Nos. 23 and 32 show Bahrām Gūr and Iskandar taking possession of their crowns, so that a link is implied between legitimacy of rule and its active acquisition. This theme is supported more generally by the large proportion of illustrations given to the *Iskandarnāma*. The double-pages in this book are clearly significant, Nos. 29 and 30 showing the benign patronage of the king and Nos. 43 and 44 making a topical reference to Akbar's magnanimity at Kandahar; it also seems possible that the missing pictures, Nos. 27 and 28, might have formed a double-page illustrating Iskandar's defeat of the Zangīs which could refer to Akbar's conquests in Rajasthan in the 1560s.

A theme, unexpected though clearly important, is the sometimes painful relation of fathers and sons, found in Nos. 5, 14, 16, 18, 20. Why Akbar should wish to dwell on this is not clear, but it may be that he sought to assuage his familial anxieties by reflecting that the problem was universal.

Subjects in whose selection Akbar must have found himself at one with his painters are those which show painters at work, Nos. 25 and 35, to which Dawlat's picture was eventually to be added. The topic of painting is also introduced into subjects where it is not strictly required, in the portrayal of pictures in Nos. 4 and 40; the pictures shown, predominantly European in character, are surely a reflection of what had newly come to hand in the royal workshop. Similarly, the art of sculpture, so important in the Hindu tradition, is celebrated in Nos. 25, 36 and 44; indeed, the statue of No. 36 may be interpreted as demonstrating as much the power of art as that of magic.

However fantastic the subject, the painters' treatment of it tends to realism: absorbed by the spectacle of the Mughal court, they recreate the world of the *Khamsa*.

SUMMARY DESCRIPTION OF
MANUSCRIPT OR. 12208

ff. 325; approximately 302 × 198mm; light-brown polished paper; *nastaʿlīq* in four columns, 21 lines; laid into frames with rulings and gold ornament; added outer margin; 37 illustrations with number and ascription to artist (see below), one additional picture; six *ʿunvān*s (ff. 1b, 32b, 110b, 169b, 231b, 285b) and eight *shamsa*s (ff. 1a, 31b, 32a, 110a, 168b, 169a, 231a, 285a); lacquered covers, turned doublures to the outside.

Illustrations, including those in the Walters Art Gallery, Baltimore:

Nūshīrvān and his vizier, f. 13b (No. 1, Manohar); *Sanjar and the old woman*, f. 15b (No. 2, Laʿl); *Farīdūn and the gazelle*, f. 19a (No. 3, Mukund); *The disputing physicians*, f. 23b (No. 4, Miskīna); *Khusraw carouses*, f. 40b (No. 5, Dharmdās); *Shāpūr before Shīrīn*, f. 45b (No. 6, Mādhū); *Shāpūr brings Khusraw news of Shīrīn*, f. 52a (No. 7, Dharmdās); *Khusraw honoured by his subjects*, f. 54a (No. 8, Narsingh); *Khusraw and Shīrīn meet on the hunting field*, f. 63b (No. 9, Nānhā); *Shīrīn entertains Khusraw*, f. 65a (No. 10, Farrukh Chela and Dhanrāj); *Khusraw defeats Bahrām Chūbīn*, f. 72a (No. 11, Manohar); *Farhād before Khusraw*, WAG, 613, f. 5a (No. 12, Sānvala); *Khusraw goes hunting*, f. 82a (No. 13, Khvāja ʿAbd al-Ṣamad); *Khusraw consults Buzurg Umīd about Shīrūya*, f. 99b (No. 14, Maddū Chela); *Shīrīn kills herself at Khusraw's tomb*, f. 102a (No. 15, Dharmdās); *Niẓāmī gives his son to the son of the Shirvānshāh*, f. 117a (No. 16, Khem Karan); *Majnūn answers his father*, f. 153b (No. 20, Nand Gvāliyārī); *Battle of the tribes*, f. 159a (No. 21, Nānhā); *Majnūn mourns his father's death*, f. 132a (No. 18, Manohar); *Majnūn visited by his mother and uncle*, f. 150b (No. 19, Sānvala); *Laylā and Majnūn faint*, f. 123a (No. 17, Farrukh Chela); *The death of Majnūn on Laylā's grave*, f. 165b (No. 22, Sūr Gujarātī); *Bahrām Gūr takes the crown of Iran*, f. 184b (No. 23, Mukund); *The king carried off by a bird*, f. 195a (No. 24, Dharmdās); *The princess paints a self-portrait*, f. 206a (No. 25, Jaganāth); *The young man who sees ladies bathing in his garden*, f. 220a (No. 26, Sānvala); *Iskandar watches the invention of mirrors*, WAG, 613, f. 16b (No. 29, Nānhā), f. 17a (No. 30, Shīvdās); *Iskandar and the dying Dārā*, WAG, 613, f. 26b (No. 31, Dharmdās); *Iskandar assumes the crown of Iran*, WAG, 613, f. 34a (No. 32, Bem Gujarātī); *Iskandar and Nūshāba entertained*, f. 244b (No. 33, Bhūra); *Iskandar shown gifts from the Kayd*, f. 254a (No. 34, Dharmdās); *Mānī paints a dead dog*, f. 262b (No. 35, Sūr Gujarātī); *The talisman that causes the Qipchāq women to veil themselves*, f. 266b (No. 36, Mukund); *The champion of Rūs wounds an elephant*, f. 273a (No. 37, Farrukh Chela); *Khiżr washes Iskandar's horse in the Water of Life*, f. 281a (No. 38, Kanak Sing Chela); *Māriya and the would-be alchemists*, f. 294a (No. 39, Sānvala); *Aflāṭūn charms the animals*, f. 298a (No. 40, Maddū Khāna-zād); *Iskandar and the seven philosophers*, f. 305a (No. 41, Nānhā); *Iskandar crossing the 'Race of Death'*, f. 312b (No. 42, Bem Gujarātī); *The priestess of Kandahar beseeches Iskandar to spare an idol*, f. 317b (No. 43, Laʿl), f. 318a (No. 44, Mukund).

Marginal detail, man with a book, f. 169b.

BIBLIOGRAPHY

Niẓāmī: C. A. Storey and François de Blois, *Persian Literature, a bio-bibliographical Survey*, Vol. V/2, London, 1994, pp. 438–95; **Akbar:** V. A. Smith, *Akbar the Great Mogul, 1542–1605*, repr. New Delhi, 1966; Michael Brand and Glenn D. Lowry, *Akbar's India: Art from the Mughal City of Victory*, New York, 1985.

Translations and summaries of texts: MA: Gholām Hosein Dārāb, *Makhzanol-Asrār: the Treasury of Mysteries of Nezāmi of Ganjeh*, London, 1945; Djamchid Mortazavi, *Nezamî de Gandjeh: le trésor des secrets*, Paris, 1987; **KS, LM, HP:** Peter J. Chelkowski, *Mirror of the Invisible World: Tales from the Khamseh of Nizami*, New York, 1975; **KS:** Henri Massé, *Nizâmi: le roman de Chosroès et Chîrîn*, Paris, 1970; **LM:** E. Mattin and G. Hill tr. from R. Gelpke, *Nizami, The Story of Layla and Majnun*, London, 1966; **HP:** 1995; C. E. Wilson, *The Haft Paikar (. . .)*, vol. I Translation, London, 1924; E. and G. Hill tr. from R. Gelpke, *Nizami: the story of the Seven Princesses*, London, 1976; Julie Scott Meisami, *Nizami: Haft Paykar, A Medieval Persian Romance*, Oxford; **IN:** Captain H. Wilberforce Clarke, *The Sikandar Nāma,e barā or Book of Alexander the Great (. . .)*, London, 1881; J. Christoph Bürgel, *Nizami: das Alexanderbuch: Iskandarname*, Zürich, 1991.

Manuscript: F. R. Martin, *The Miniature Paintings and Painters of Persia, India and Turkey, from the 8th to the 18th Century*, London, 1912; Sir George Warner, *Descriptive Catalogue of illuminated Manuscripts in the Library of C. W. Dyson Perrins, DCL, FSA*, 2 vols, Oxford, 1920; Percy Brown, *Indian Painting under the Mughals, A.D. 1550 to A.D. 1750*, Oxford, 1924; Stuart Cary Welch, 'The Emperor Akbar's *Khamsa* of Niẓāmī', *Journal of the Walters Art Gallery*, XXIII, 1960, pp. 87–96; T. J. Brown, G. M. Meredith-Owens, and D. H. Turner, 'Manuscripts from the Dyson Perrins Collection', *The British Museum Quarterly*, XXIII/2, 1961, pp. 28–30 and pl. XV; G. M. Meredith-Owens, *Handlist of Persian Manuscripts 1895–1966*, London, 1968; Norah M. Titley, *Miniatures from Persian Manuscripts (. . .) in the British Library and the British Museum*, London, 1977; Jeremiah P. Losty, *The Art of the Book in India*, London, 1982.

Front cover: Shapur brings Khrusraw news of Shīrīn (f. 52a detail)
Back cover: f. 59 (detail)
Half title: Akbar or Jahān Gīr (Add. Or 1039)
Title page: Chinoiserie (f. 230b)